W9-AWK-865

The
United Nations

Global Leadership

Pioneering International Law

Conventions, Treaties, and Standards

by Sheila Nelson

Mason Crest Publishers

Philadelphia

Mason Crest Publishers Inc.
370 Reed Road
Broomall, Pennsylvania 19008
(866) MCP-BOOK (toll free)

First printing
1 2 3 4 5 6 7 8 9 10

Library of Congress Cataloging-in-Publication Data

Nelson, Sheila.
  Pioneering international law : conventions, treaties, and standards / by Sheila Nelson.
     p. cm. — (The United Nations—global leadership)
  Includes bibliographical references and index.
  ISBN 1-4222-0073-6   ISBN 1-4222-0065-5 (series)
  1. International law—History. 2. United Nations. 3. Pacific settlement of international disputes.
4. Terrorism. I. Title. II. Series.
  KZ1242.N45 2007
  341.09—dc22
                             2006001498

Interior design by Benjamin Stewart.
Interiors produced by Harding House Publishing Service, Inc.
www.hardinghousepages.com
Cover design by Peter Culatta.
Printed in the Hashemite Kingdom of Jordan.

Contents

Introduction
by Dr. Bruce Russett

The United Nations was founded in 1945 by the victors of World War II. They hoped the new organization could learn from the mistakes of the League of Nations that followed World War I—and prevent another war.

The United Nations has not been able to bring worldwide peace; that would be an unrealistic hope. But it has contributed in important ways to the world's experience of more than sixty years without a new world war. Despite its flaws, the United Nations has contributed to peace.

Like any big organization, the United Nations is composed of many separate units with different jobs. These units make three different kinds of contributions. The most obvious to students in North America and other democracies are those that can have a direct and immediate impact for peace.

Especially prominent is the Security Council, which is the only UN unit that can authorize the use of military force against countries and can require all UN members to cooperate in isolating an aggressor country's economy. In the Security Council, each of the big powers—Britain, China, France, Russia, and the United States—can veto any proposed action. That's because the founders of United Nations recognized that if the Council tried to take any military action against the strong opposition of a big power it would result in war. As a result, the United Nations was often sidelined during the Cold War era. Since the end of the Cold War in 1990, however, the Council has authorized many military actions, some directed against specific aggressors but most intended as more neutral peacekeeping efforts. Most of its peacekeeping efforts have been to end civil wars rather than wars between countries. Not all have succeeded, but many have. The United Nations Secretary-General also has had an important role in mediating some conflicts.

UN units that promote trade and economic development make a different kind of contribution. Some help to establish free markets for greater prosperity, or like the UN Development Programme, provide economic and technical assistance to reduce poverty in poor countries. Some are especially concerned with environmental problems or health issues. For example, the World Health Organization and UNICEF deserve great credit for eliminating the deadly disease of smallpox from the world. Poor countries especially support the United Nations for this reason. Since many wars, within and between countries, stem from economic deprivation, these efforts make an important indirect contribution to peace.

Still other units make a third contribution: they promote human rights. The High Commission for Refugees, for example, has worked to ease the distress of millions of refugees who have fled their countries to escape from war and political persecution. A special unit of the Secretary-General's office has supervised and assisted free elections in more than ninety countries. It tries to establish stable and democratic governments in newly independent countries or in countries where the people have defeated a dictatorial government. Other units promote the rights of women, children, and religious and ethnic minorities. The General Assembly provides a useful setting for debate on these and other issues.

These three kinds of action—to end violence, to reduce poverty, and to promote social and political justice—all make a contribution to peace. True peace requires all three, working together.

The UN does not always succeed: like individuals, it makes mistakes . . . and it often learns from its mistakes. Despite the United Nations' occasional stumbles, over the years it has grown and moved forward. These books will show you how.

The United Nations' headquarters in New York City

Chapter **1**

The United Nations and International Law: An Overview

W hat happens when nations disagree with each other? Whose laws do they follow, and who decides the outcome? International law deals with these and other kinds of questions concerning international issues.

The International Court of Justice in session in The Hague

From the Charter of the United Nations

The International Court of Justice shall be the principal judicial organ of the United Nations. It shall function in accordance with the annexed Statute, which is based upon the Statute of the Permanent Court of International Justice and forms an integral part of the present Charter. . . .

Each Member of the United Nations undertakes to comply with the decision of the International Court of Justice in any case to which it is a party.

If any party to a case fails to perform the obligations incumbent upon it under a judgment rendered by the Court, the other party may have recourse to the Security Council, which may, if it deems necessary, make recommendations or decide upon measures to be taken to give effect to the judgment.

The United Nations has always been involved with international law, ever since its creation in 1945 after the end of the Second World War. The UN's main goals are to prevent war and to help the peoples of the world live better, more fulfilling lives. Through the treaties and conventions of international law, the United Nations works to accomplish these goals.

Issues of International Law

Some of the disputes that arise concerning international law involve violations of treaties. Others concern disagreements between nations or between international organizations or corporations. These disagreements can include disputes as to where the sea borders between countries lie and whether a nation or international business is violating international environmental standards.

While the term "international law" usually refers to laws governing the relationships between nations or international organizations, it can also include laws overseeing war crimes and crimes against humanity.

International Court of Justice

Shortly after its founding, the United Nations established the International Court of Justice (ICJ)—sometimes called the World Court. The ICJ is one of the six principal organs of the United

Pioneering International Law: Conventions, Treaties, and Standards

Nations, and its main job is to settle legal disputes between nations, as well as to offer nonbinding legal opinions to international organizations that request them. The UN's participation in international law is primarily through the ICJ, although the Security Council is actively involved in conflict resolution.

The ICJ meets at the Peace Palace in The Hague, the Netherlands. The court is composed of fifteen judges, each from a different country. These judges are elected by the UN General Assembly and Security Council and serve for nine years, after which they may be reelected. Every three years, one-third of the judges are eligible for reelection.

All countries that are members of the United Nations are also members of the ICJ. This means that all UN members have agreed to abide by the decisions of the ICJ. All decisions of the ICJ are binding and without *appeal*.

Many of the cases brought before the ICJ deal with *breaches* in treaties or disputed borders. A number of international treaties made after the founding of the United Nations state that if a disagreement concerning the treaty arises, and the disagreement cannot be resolved another way, the ICJ will have jurisdiction to settle the issue.

The Peace Palace in The Hague, where the ICJ meets

The UN's Security Council is also actively involved with international conflict resolution.

Russia's gift to the United Nations, a statue titled Let Us Beat Swords into Ploughshares, *refers to a verse in the Hebrew scriptures. Unfortunately, the United Nations often lacks the power to carry out its lofty ideals.*

Challenges to International Law

Although the decisions of the ICJ are theoretically binding, the court has no way to ensure its verdicts are carried out. Even though all members of the United Nations agreed when they signed the UN Charter to submit to the jurisdiction of the ICJ, in reality this does not always occur. If countries do not voluntarily agree to follow the rulings of the ICJ, the court must then ask the Security Council to enforce the verdict. The Security Council can then decide to cut off diplomatic relations with the offending nation or to enforce economic *sanctions* against them, such as encouraging other UN members to cut off trade relations.

The UN Charter first went into effect in 1942.

In the 1980s, the United States illegally invaded the small country of Nicaragua.

This problem is compounded when the offending country is a permanent member of the UN Security Council. The Security Council has five permanent members—China, France, Russia, the United Kingdom, and the United States—and each permanent member has the right to **_veto_** any proposal. This means that if the Security Council were to order one of the permanent members to carry out an ICJ decision, that nation could simply refuse and then veto any proposed sanctions. A similar situation happened in 1984, when the ICJ ordered the United States to withdraw from Nicaragua and to pay compensation for illegally invading the country. Although the United States eventually pulled out of Nicaragua, it refused to pay any money as compensation. The Security Council could not force the United States to follow the rulings of the ICJ, since the United States was a permanent member and had veto power. The United States claimed the ICJ had no jurisdiction over it and that it was not bound by the decision.

While the United Nations is involved in many of the international law decisions today, international law has existed for a much longer time.

It was considered a terrible crime in World War I when German forces falsely used a white flag to lure the Allied forces into the open.

Chapter **2**

Development and Codification of International Law

International law has existed for thousands of years—nearly as long as nations have existed. Long ago, matters of international law were often not written down, but instead were understood as a matter of honor. For example, people considered it a horrible offense to attack while under the ***flag of parley***. The earliest examples of written international law were treaties drawn up between nations. Usually, the treaty would state that the two nations would be allies and each would defend the other if it were attacked.

Henri Dunant, a Swiss businessman, proved that one person can make a long-lasting difference to the world.

Chapter Two—Development and Codification of International Law

The Geneva Conventions

In 1859, a Swiss businessman named Henri Dunant was in the Italian town of Solferino when a battle between French-Piedmontese and Austrian forces broke out. Dunant was horrified when he saw how the wounded from both sides were simply left to die on the battlefield. He recruited people from the nearby villages to help the wounded, insisting they aid those from both armies without distinction.

In the years after the battle, Dunant began to work to establish a group to impartially help the wounded during battles. By 1864, the Geneva Society for Public Welfare had become interested in Dunant's idea. They founded a committee that later became the International Committee of the Red Cross and held the first Geneva Convention, with representatives from sixteen European countries attending. The result was the Convention for the ***Amelioration*** of the Condition of the Wounded in Armies in the Field, a treaty protecting ambulances and medical personnel during wartime.

Three more Geneva Conventions added treaties dealing with the treatment of naval forces (1906), prisoners of war (1929), and civilians during wartime (1949). Together, these agreements helped define what most believed to be ethical conduct during times of war.

From the Geneva Protocol

Whereas the use in war of asphyxiating, poisonous or other gases, and of all analogous liquids, materials or devices, has been justly condemned by the general opinion of the civilised world; and

Whereas the prohibition of such use has been declared in Treaties to which the majority of Powers of the world are Parties; and

To the end that this prohibition shall be universally accepted as a part of International Law, binding alike the conscience and the practice of nations;

Declare:

That the High Contracting Parties, so far as they are not already Parties to Treaties prohibiting such use, accept this prohibition, agree to extend this prohibition to the use of bacteriological methods of warfare and agree to be bound as between themselves according to the terms of this declaration.

Pioneering International Law: Conventions, Treaties, and Standards

Aerial battles came to be an accepted form of warfare during World War II.

The Hague Conventions

Other treaties dealing with the laws of war were the Hague Conventions, signed during the First and Second Peace Conferences at The Hague, in the Netherlands. The first Hague Convention was held in 1899 and set out specific guidelines for behavior during wartime. Included were laws against launching explosives from balloons and against the use of poison gas.

The second Hague Convention, held in 1907, expanded the principles set out in the first convention. One section stated that countries must not begin hostilities without a formal declaration of war, both to the other party and to neutral countries. Another banned the use of automatic underwater mines, in the interest of protecting commercial ships.

During World War I, some of the agreements originally set out in the Hague Conventions were ignored—such as those forbidding aerial bombardments and the use of poison gas. While aerial bombardments did come to be an accepted means of waging war, use of poison gas against enemy forces continued to be outlawed.

In 1925, the Geneva Protocol—formally called "The Protocol for the Prohibition of the Use in War of Asphyxiating, Poisonous or other Gases, and of Bacteriological Methods of Warfare"—

During World War I, the Hague Conventions' ban on poison gas was ignored.

The Permanent Court of Arbitration is housed in the Peace Palace in The Hague, along with the International Court of Justice.

restated the ban against chemical and biological warfare. The Biological Weapons Convention of 1972 and the Chemical Weapons Convention of 1993 also continued and extended the international agreements.

Permanent Court of Arbitration

The first act of the First Peace Convention at The Hague in 1899 was to establish a Permanent Court of Arbitration. The court, now housed in the Peace Palace at The Hague together with the ICJ, would allow disputing nations a neutral setting in which to have their differences heard.

Today, the Permanent Court of Arbitration is, according to its Web site, "perfectly situated at the juncture between public and private international law to meet the rapidly evolving dispute resolution needs of the international community." The court now "administers **arbitration, conciliation** and fact finding in disputes involving various combinations of states, private parties and intergovernmental organizations."

The Permanent Court of Arbitration has sought to bring resolution to the world's military conflicts.

The League of Nations' council room in Geneva, Switzerland

Chapter Two—Development and Codification of International Law

The United Nations and the Development of International Law

Even before the creation of the United Nations, the League of Nations had begun setting up procedures to establish international laws. In 1924, the League of Nations resolved to create the Committee of Experts for the Progressive Codification of International Law. The committee would have seventeen members who would study international legal concerns and bring forward issues they felt should be addressed by the Assembly of the League of Nations. Although the League did not make great progress toward the *codification* of international law, the committee became the forerunner of international law under the United Nations.

The International Law Commission of the United Nations was founded in 1947, only two years after the establishment of the United Nations itself. The purpose of the commission is to study matters of international law and to write recommendations. These recommendations are then passed on to the UN's General Assembly for discussion and the possibility of becoming law. To become law, a recommendation—draft article—must be written into the form of a convention- or treaty—and UN member nations are then given the opportunity to sign it.

The field of international law develops constantly, with new treaties and agreements being added as they are needed. New technologies and shifting political dynamics often call for updated laws. While international law sets out guidelines for the relationships between nations, conflicts often arise over the interpretation of these laws. The United Nations has become a world leader in conflict resolution, helping nations overcome these differences to live in peace with each other.

The United Nations works to bring an end to military conflicts.

The United Nations' Role in Conflict Resolution

Any time more than one person is involved, disagreements will certainly happen from time to time. When countries are involved, with their differing cultures and worldviews, these disagreements can sometimes be magnified into wars or other international hostilities.

UNDOF troops sweep for mines.

Chapter Three—The United Nations' Role in Conflict Resolution

The United Nations was created to prevent war and to help people live better lives. To do this, the organization set up methods to help disputing nations end their disagreements. The Charter of the United Nations states that one of the main purposes of the United Nations is

> to maintain international peace and security, and to that end: to take effective collective measures for the prevention and removal of threats to the peace, and for the suppression of acts of aggression or other breaches of the peace, and to bring about by peaceful means, and in conformity with the principles of justice and international law, adjustment or settlement of international disputes or situations which might lead to a breach of the peace.

When conflicts do arise, the United Nations can help in a number of ways. One way is to offer the ICJ as a place where nations can have their differences heard. The differing parties agree to follow the rulings of the court. Another way is through peacekeeping missions.

Peacekeeping

From its beginning, the United Nations wanted to help keep peace in the world. In 1948, following the Arab-Israeli War, the United Nations set up its first peacekeeping mission, known as the United Nations Truce Supervision Organization (UNTSO)—a mission still continuing as of 2005. The term "peacekeeping" was not used at the time, however.

UN peacekeeping officially began in 1956, during the Suez Crisis. Canadian diplomat Lester Pearson proposed to the UN secretary-general and the General Assembly that the United Nations create an emergency police force to resolve the situation. Pearson's idea was for UN troops to physically stand between warring parties and force the return of peace. The result was UNEF I, the

United Nations Peacekeeping Operations

peacekeeping operations since 1948: 60
current peace operations: 18
total number of personnel serving in peacekeeping operations: 84,409
total number of fatalities in peacekeeping operations since 1948: 2,028

(as of October 31, 2005; taken from the UN Peacekeeping Web site)

First United Nations Emergency Force. UNEF I became the first armed peacekeeping mission of the United Nations, creating a pattern for dozens more missions over the next fifty years. In general, peacekeepers do not fight—and, in fact, are not always armed—but act as a neutral presence in a tense situation, allowing ***diplomatic*** solutions to be carried out. The peacekeeping forces also help both sides follow through with the peaceful solutions on which they have agreed. This includes assistance with setting up political elections, economic development, and restoring national order.

Peacemaking

Similar to peacekeeping is peacemaking. While the goal of both is an end to hostilities, peacekeeping involves the use of a UN police force. Peacemaking, on the other hand, generally works through diplomatic channels to find a solution to the conflict.

Peacemaking involves mediation. This means that a neutral third party sits down with the

UNEF troops on patrol in Egypt in 1957

The blue helmet is worn by UN peacekeepers.

U Thant was the UN's third secretary-general.

disputing parties and helps them to work out an answer to the problem. During mediation, both sides agree to listen to the mediator and to try and find a solution acceptable to both. The United Nations is often able to help negotiate resolutions to disagreements between nations. Sometimes the UN secretary-general acts directly in peacemaking situations, although he usually appoints other high-ranking UN officials to act on his behalf.

The United Nations often tries to work closely with regional organizations when involved in the process of peacemaking. These organizations are generally more familiar with local situations and can help with peace negotiations.

One example of United Nations peacemaking took place in Angola. In the late 1970s, civil war broke out in Angola between several factions. After a number of attempts at peace, the two main sides of the conflict, UNITA and MPLA, agreed to a UN-brokered peace deal in 1994, called the Lusaka Protocol. Four years later, the peace crumbled, and fighting broke out again. This time, the

A young UNITA soldier in Angola

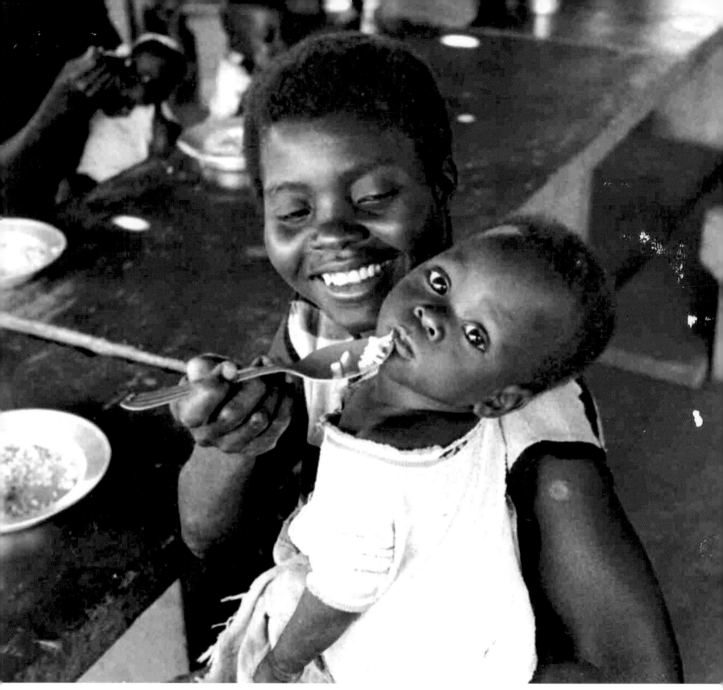

The United Nations works with nongovernmental agencies to help build peace in war-torn regions. Here Relief Web distributes food to children in Angola.

hostilities lasted until 2002, when the leader of UNITA, Jonas Savimbi, was assassinated. The other members of UNITA agreed to stop the fighting and instead become the government opposition party. In 2005, the Angolan president, José Eduardo dos Santos, announced that the country would hold elections in 2006, the first since 1992. Throughout the UN peacemaking process of establishing stable diplomatic relations between the warring sides, UN peacekeeping troops were also in place, making sure the cease-fires were maintained.

Peace-Building

A third step in conflict resolution, coming after peacekeeping and peacemaking, is peace-building. Peace-building refers to the process of helping nations rebuild after long periods of war or violent unrest. This is often a long-term procedure that can involve bringing refugees back into the country and helping them reestablish normal lives, setting up political structures and elections, and helping nations transition from a highly militarized state to a stable and thriving country.

Another aspect of peace-building involves helping two nations, or two groups of people within a nation, to learn to live together peacefully. Usually, many prejudices and *stereotypes* have developed during times of hostility. Peace-building helps both sides develop normal relationships with the other. Education and information distribution are used to help people find things in common with their former enemies. Joint rebuilding projects using people from each side of the previous conflict can be very helpful in forming bonds and friendships. When people work closely together for a common cause, they often find themselves respecting and appreciating each other.

The United Nations is involved at all levels of the conflict resolution process, from peacekeeping troops physically standing between two warring sides to the long-reaching efforts of peace-building. One very specific type of conflict involves incidents taking place at sea, in international waters. A large body of international laws known as maritime law governs these conflicts.

Ships at sea are ruled by maritime law.

Chapter

4

Maritime Law

No single country governs the oceans, so who decides what happens when disagreements arise between ships at sea? Maritime law, part of the larger body of international law, has developed over thousands of years to deal with questions such as this.

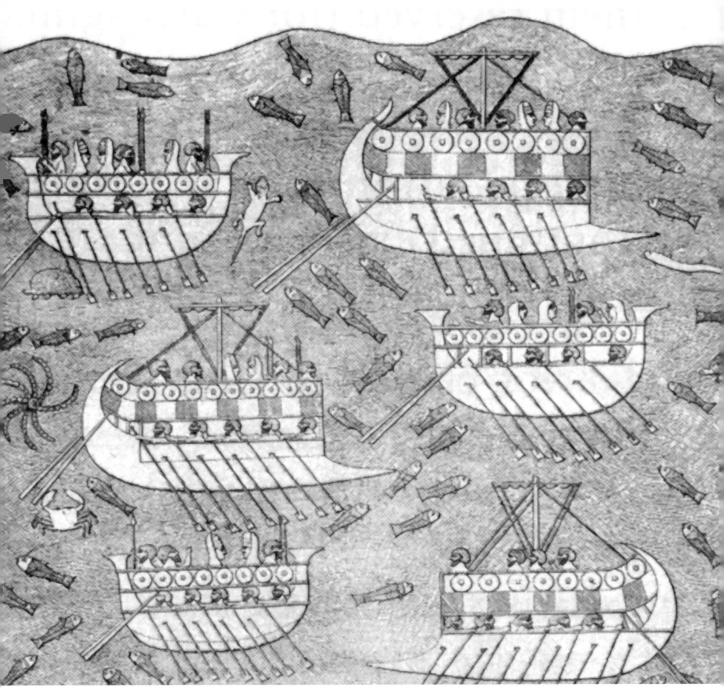

Early Phoenician sailors helped build the foundation of maritime law.

History of Maritime Law

The earliest known examples of maritime law are laws dealing with disputes on the Mediterranean Sea between Egyptian, Greek, and Phoenician ships. The Mediterranean was heavily traveled by ships carrying trade goods. With so many ships traveling a small area, arguments often arose concerning things such as lost freight or collisions between ships. The countries involved, following a pattern established by the Greek island of Rhodes, set up courts at each port specifically designed to deal with questions of disputes at sea. The decisions passed down by these courts gradually became formalized into maritime law. When the Romans grew into power, they adopted these laws and continued them, spreading them north as they explored and expanded their territory.

During the Middle Ages, European nations developed maritime law to deal with the issues they faced. In general, these were very much like the issues facing ancient Phoenician sailors on the Mediterranean Sea. For example, a problem facing both ancient and medieval sailors was piracy. Maritime law tried to set in place laws dealing with pirates and pirate attacks, allowing pirates to be captured and tried.

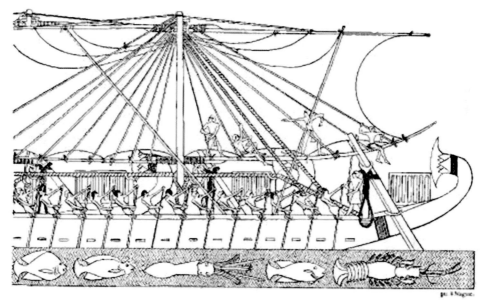

An early Egyptian ship

From the United Nations Convention on the Law of the Sea, preamble

Prompted by the desire to settle, in a spirit of mutual understanding and cooperation, all issues relating to the law of the sea and aware of the historic significance of this Convention as an important contribution to the maintenance of peace, justice and progress for all peoples of the world. . . ,

Conscious that the problems of ocean space are closely interrelated and need to be considered as a whole,

Recognizing the desirability of establishing through this Convention, with due regard for the sovereignty of all States, a legal order for the seas and oceans which will facilitate international communication, and will promote the peaceful uses of the seas and oceans, the equitable and efficient utilization of their resources, the conservation of their living resources, and the study, protection and preservation of the marine environment. . . ,

Believing that the codification and progressive development of the law of the sea achieved in this Convention will contribute to the strengthening of peace, security, cooperation and friendly relations among all nations in conformity with the principles of justice and equal rights and will promote the economic and social advancement of all peoples of the world, in accordance with the Purposes and Principles of the United Nations as set forth in the Charter. . . .

Today, many of the maritime laws have developed from laws created hundreds of years ago. New laws have been added, however, to address environmental concerns and the use of modern technologies.

Freedom of the Seas

In the seventeenth century, as more and more ships began to travel across the open oceans, the principle of "freedom of the seas" developed. People believed the oceans belonged to everyone equally and should not be claimed by individual nations. Territorial limits were restricted to three **nautical miles** off shore.

During the seventeenth century, the oceans seemed like a vast region of boundless freedom.

Piracy is often looked at as a long-ago fantasy—but it is actually—a modern-day problem.

Modern Pirates

Blackbeard . . . Calico Jack . . . Black Bart: we usually think of pirates as having lived centuries ago, flying the Jolly Roger skull and crossbones flag and sailing the high seas in a masted sailing ship. These pirates would wave a cutlass, wear an eye patch, and maybe have a wooden leg. Today, pirates still exist, but the reality is much different.

Modern pirates are very active in some parts of the world's seas, for example near Southeast Asia or South America. These pirates typically use small motor boats and machine guns. They coordinate their attacks using cell phones, then come alongside slower cargo ships or recreational boats, and steal money and possessions from the crew. At times pirates will also steal the ship itself, setting the crew adrift and repainting the vessel to disguise it from law enforcement officers.

Prosecuting pirates can be difficult, since they often operate in international waters. However, since piracy is considered a crime against humanity, few countries will protect pirates against prosecution.

The idea of freedom of the seas lasted for three hundred years, but in the twentieth century, problems began to arise. New technologies allowed companies to begin drilling the ocean floor for oil, while fishing ships hovered just outside the three-mile limit and scooped up their catch. Pollution also became a problem, with countries complaining about ships leaking fuel and debris that flowed into their waters and onto their shores.

The League of Nations, in 1930, recognized the need for an adjustment to the freedom of the seas concept, but made no steps toward changing the situation. In 1945, however, American president Harry Truman extended the territorial waters of the United States to include all natural resources on the *continental shelf*. The distance the continental shelf extends away from land varies widely, from almost nothing to over nine hundred miles, but on average it is approximately forty-eight miles wide. Over the next five years, Argentina, Chile, Peru, and Ecuador all followed the example of the United States and claimed the waters out to a two-hundred-nautical-mile limit. A number of other nations decided soon afterward to extend their territorial rights out to a twelve-nautical-mile limit.

United Nations Convention on the Law of the Sea

In 1956, the United Nations held the First United Nations Conference on Law of the Sea (UNCLOS I). A second followed in 1960, and a third (UNCLOS III) lasted from 1973 until 1982. Although UNCLOS I made important steps in extending the territorial waters of coastal nations and in defining the rights of ships on open seas, the most important steps were made at UNCLOS III. On December 10, 1982, the United Nations Convention on the Law of the Sea was opened for signatures. Twelve years later, in 1994, the convention went into effect with the signing of the sixtieth nation.

The convention acts as a constitution governing the oceans of the world. One of its most important features was the creation of the EEZs—Exclusive Economic Zones. While the convention gave each coastal nation a territorial limit of twelve nautical miles, it also gave these nations a further two hundred nautical miles as an EEZ (unless this would extend into the waters of another nation). Countries can patrol their territorial waters, boarding ships to enforce national laws as necessary, but the further distance added by the EEZ gives control over all natural resources out to the two-hundred-mile limit. Coastal nations can use the resources within these zones as they see fit, and they are also responsible for their conservation. The resources controlled within the EEZs include the rights to all oil, gas, and minerals, as well as fishing rights. This means, in effect, that, generally, international fishing boats cannot legally fish within two hundred and twelve nautical miles of another country's coastline.

Pollution has become such an intrusive problem that a major part of the United Nations Convention on the Law of the Sea deals with concerns of conservation and the challenges posed by new technologies. Each coastal nation is authorized—and encouraged—to put in place antipollution laws dealing with activities both at sea and on land. The conservation of fish stocks and other marine life is also strongly encouraged. In 2002, the United Nations World Summit on Sustainable Development, held in Johannesburg, South Africa, discussed the need for protection of the earth's oceans and marine life. Goals set out at this *summit* included maintaining or rebuilding depleted fish stocks and combating illegal or unregulated fishing.

International Seabed Authority

In 1994, when the United Nations Convention on the Law of the Sea went into effect, the International Seabed Authority was officially established. The creation of the authority had been set out in the 1982 convention and consequently took effect along with it. Although a UN treaty created the authority, it operates from Kingston, Jamaica, as an independent body.

Nations have control over their coastal resources.

Pioneering International Law: Conventions, Treaties, and Standards

The International Seabed Authority governs the resources of the sea floor in areas not included in any national waters, specifically mineral resources. The authority allows private companies to apply for exploration and mining rights on the sea floor and also puts laws in place to govern such activities. In 2000, the authority established guidelines governing the exploration for *polymetallic nodules* found on the ocean floor and accepted contracts from several companies interested in such exploration.

The main problem with deep-sea mining is the cost. Reaching and gathering minerals found over a mile below the surface of the ocean is extremely difficult and expensive. Most companies considering underwater mining have decided the benefits do not outweigh the costs. Generally, it is much cheaper to conduct mining on land than it is to explore deep-sea options, despite the fact that land mining means working around human populations. While a number of companies are interested in taking up deep-sea mineral exploration sometime in the future, very few feel technologies have become advanced enough to make the effort profitable.

International Tribunal for the Law of the Sea

The United Nations Convention on the Law of the Sea also set out detailed provisions for disputes arising in international waters. First, disputing parties are encouraged to work out the disagreement peacefully between themselves. If this fails, the convention provides four options for settlement of the problem. The options include appealing to the International Tribunal for the Law of the Sea or the ICJ, or choosing from two types of *arbitral tribunals*. Whichever option the parties choose, the decision of the court or tribunal is legally binding. If the parties cannot agree which option they should choose, they are automatically assigned an arbitral tribunal.

The International Tribunal for the Law of the Sea was created by the convention specifically to deal with such international marine disagreements. Like the International Seabed Authority, the tribunal was created by a treaty of the United Nations but now operates as an independent body. Twenty-one judges, elected from nations that are members of the convention, serve on the tribunal, meeting at its seat in Hamburg, Germany. The tribunal regulates all aspects of international waters other than the ocean floor, which is governed by the International Seabed Authority, and operates through three main bodies—the Chamber of Summary Procedure, the Chamber for Fisheries Disputes, and the Chamber for Marine Environment Disputes—as well as one special chamber created by request to address the *Case Concerning the Conservation and Sustainable Exploitation of Swordfish Stocks in the South-Eastern Pacific Ocean (Chile vs. the European Community)*.

The UN's International Seabed Authority governs undersea resources.

The United Nations has founded and cooperates with international organizations that ensure that the Earth's oceans are shared fairly by all its citizens.

Much of modern maritime law has been established by or with the help of the United Nations. In cases such as the creation of the International Seabed Authority and the International Tribunal for the Law of the Sea, the United Nations helps to establish international regulating organizations and then releases them to work independently. These bodies continue to act in cooperation with the United Nations, however.

While most international law deals with situations that have already occurred and must now be resolved, the United Nations is also involved in taking *preventive* measures.

In today's world, crime is an international problem.

Chapter

Crime Prevention

Around the world, crimes take place every day. Many of these are international crimes that cross borders. The United Nations is concerned with stopping and preventing international crime, since such illegal activities can hurt innocent people. Countries with high crime rates also have trouble becoming stable members of the international community. The UN's position on crime, as laid out in the *Compendium of United Nations Standards and Norms in Crime Prevention and Criminal Justice,* is that "crime and delinquency should not be interpreted as merely a problem of illegal behaviour and law enforcement but also as phenomena closely associated with economic and social development." In other words, the United Nations believes that by helping countries solve their economic and social problems, they will also contribute to reducing their crime.

The Centre for International Crime Prevention is located in Vienna, Austria.

The Centre for International Crime Prevention

In 1948, the United Nations founded the Centre for International Crime Prevention, based in Vienna, Austria. The Centre works with other international organizations to help prevent crimes such as arms dealing, ***money laundering***, and drug and people smuggling.

Part of the Centre's job is to gather information on crime trends and areas of the world requiring intervention. This allows governments to make informed decisions about what types of policies work and can help them plan appropriate relationships with other countries to deter crime.

Although the Centre spends a large portion of its time researching crime and criminal activities, it is also actively involved in preventing and fighting crime. Working with all levels of governments and law enforcement agencies, the Centre has three major goals: "strengthening the capacity of Governments to reform legislation and criminal justice systems; establishing institutions and mechanisms for the detection, investigation, prosecution and adjudication of various types of crimes; [and] upgrading the skills of criminal justice personnel."

Along with these goals, the Centre has focused on three main types of crime, developing global programs to address specific concerns. These are: the Global Programme on Transnational Organized Crime, the Global Programme against Trafficking in Human Beings, and the Global Programme against Corruption. Transnational organized crime usually involves many different

International Anti-Corruption Day

To help raise public awareness on issues relating to crime prevention, the United Nations Office on Drugs and Crime often holds special days devoted to educating people on a specific topic. For example, June 26, 2005, was the International Day against Drug Abuse and Illicit Trafficking. On December 9, 2005, the United Nations held the International Anti-Corruption Day. The theme for this day was "You can stop corruption." Since most people do not consider corruption anything to do with their own lives, this UN awareness campaign tries to educate the public on what corruption really means. As the campaign's Web site states,

Corruption occurs whenever parents pay teachers illegal fees to give their children an education, patients pay extra to get proper health care, citizens give public officials gifts or money to speed up procedures, and drivers bribe police officers to avoid a fine. What many see as simply a way to get things done is, in fact, a crime.

Drug trafficking reaches across borders.

crimes carried out by criminal organizations. These crimes can include drug trafficking, arms dealing, money laundering, or counterfeiting. Human trafficking is a form of slavery, in which people are either kidnapped or lured into captivity and then forced to work for their captors. Corruption involves a misuse of power by people in authority to benefit themselves at the expense of others. While this often refers to the activities of government leaders or those in top-level business positions, ordinary people can also become involved in corruption when they bribe someone in authority to gain favors or to stay out of trouble.

The United Nations Office on Drugs and Crime

Even though the Centre for International Crime Prevention was created in 1948, it now functions under the authority of a much newer and larger organization, the United Nations Office on Drugs

Arms dealing and drug trafficking often go hand-in-hand.

The Commission on Crime Prevention and Criminal Justice works to bring justice to the entire planet.

and Crime (UNODC), founded in 1997. The UNODC oversees a number of smaller groups, all associated with areas of crime prevention or fighting. Besides the Centre for International Crime Prevention, the UNODC also administers the United Nations Drug Control Programme and the Terrorism Prevention Branch.

Like the Centre for International Crime Prevention, the UNODC spends a large part of its time on research and analysis, studying crime problems and trends. Apart from research, the UNODC also works with governments to encourage them to sign international treaties setting crime-prevention goals and standards. Lastly, it works directly with law enforcement and crime-prevention groups to provide training and help with cutting crime rates.

The Commission on Crime Prevention and Criminal Justice

While most organizations working under the UNODC—such as the Centre for International Crime Prevention—work directly with governments and agencies to analyze and prevent crime, the Commission on Crime Prevention and Criminal Justice deals more with the legal side of crime prevention. The commission is made up of representatives from forty countries who meet once a year in the spring to discuss matters of international criminal law. The job of the commission is to put together international policies on responses to crime. The Centre for International Crime Prevention is then given the task of carrying out these policies and educating governments about them.

When the commission was created in 1992, it was given four areas to focus on: "international action to combat national and transnational crime, including organized crime, economic crime and money laundering; promoting the role of criminal law in protecting the environment; crime prevention in urban areas, including juvenile crime and violence; and improving the efficiency and fairness of criminal justice administration systems." At each annual session, the commission discusses one or more of these areas. The commission then reports to its administering body, the Economic and Social Council, which assists in preparing decisions that the Centre of International Crime Prevention carries out.

United Nations Crime Congresses

Every five years, the United Nations holds an international convention on crime, officially called the United Nations Congress on the Prevention of Crime and the Treatment of Offenders. The United Nations first began holding these crime congresses in 1955, following a pattern set by the

Pioneering International Law: Conventions, Treaties, and Standards

International Penal and Penitentiary Commission beginning in 1885. Delegates from all over the world attend the conventions, together with experts on crime and members of crime prevention and criminal justice organizations.

During the Eleventh UN Crime Congress, held in Bangkok, Thailand, in April of 2005, the attendees discussed transnational organized crime, terrorism, and corruption. Participants were also offered the chance to attend a number of workshops on topics such as economic crime and computer-related crime.

The crime congresses are important because they bring high-ranking officials and experts together to talk about issues relating to crime, but also because it is at the crime congresses where United Nations Conventions—international treaties—on crime are first presented and discussed.

United Nations Crime and Drug Conventions

The first UN Conventions related to crime were the drug control treaties. The first of these was the Single Convention on Narcotic Drugs, 1961. The purpose of this treaty was to limit who had

Computer technology makes it easier for crimes to cross borders.

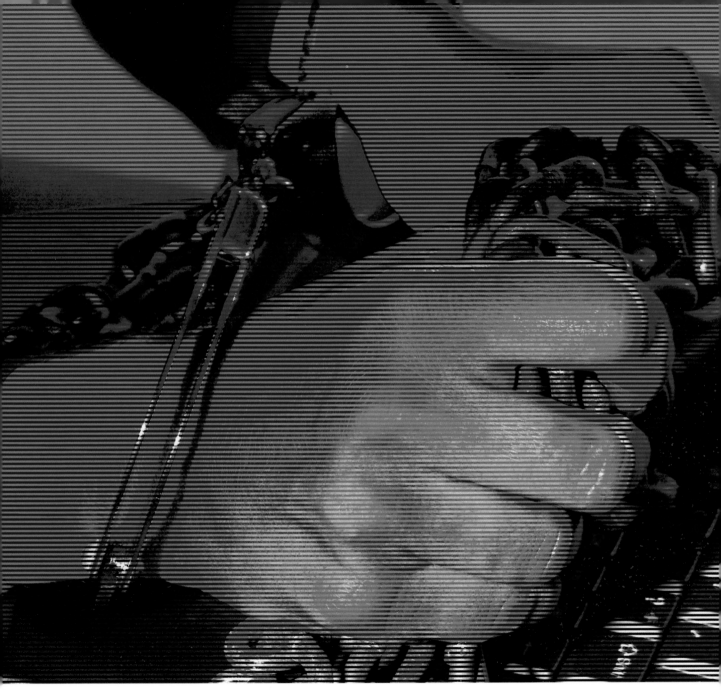

Regulating the Internet is one of the challenges facing recent UN crime congresses.

The Convention against Transnational Organized Crime seeks to control the manufacture and traffic of ammunition.

legal access to drugs and to fight drug smuggling. In 1971, the Convention on Psychotropic Substances expanded the definition of illegal drugs. Finally, in 1988, the Convention against the Illicit Traffic in Narcotic Drugs and Psychotropic Substances set up ***extradition*** laws relating to drug traffickers.

More recently, the United Nations has crafted two more crime-related conventions, the Convention against Transnational Organized Crime, which took effect in 2003, and the Convention against Corruption, which went into effect late in 2005. Although each treaty was drafted several years before taking effect, a certain number of nations must sign and ***ratify*** the document before it becomes official.

The Convention against Transnational Organized Crime has three protocols attached to it as well, supplemental treaties that go into further detail on certain issues. These protocols are: The Protocol to Prevent, Suppress and Punish Trafficking in Persons, Especially Women and Children; The Protocol against the Smuggling of Migrants by Land, Air and Sea; and The Protocol against the Illicit Manufacturing of and Trafficking in Firearms, Their Parts and Components and Ammunition.

The United Nations, as an international organization, is often involved in creating international policies. This means setting standards on criminal behavior and studying the best ways to prevent crime. Equipped with information on crime trends around the world, agencies such as the UNODC can help in creating international treaties to combat criminal activity.

Recently, many people have become aware of the dangers the crime of terrorism could pose to their everyday life. In response, the United Nations has devoted a significant portion of its resources to combating this threat.

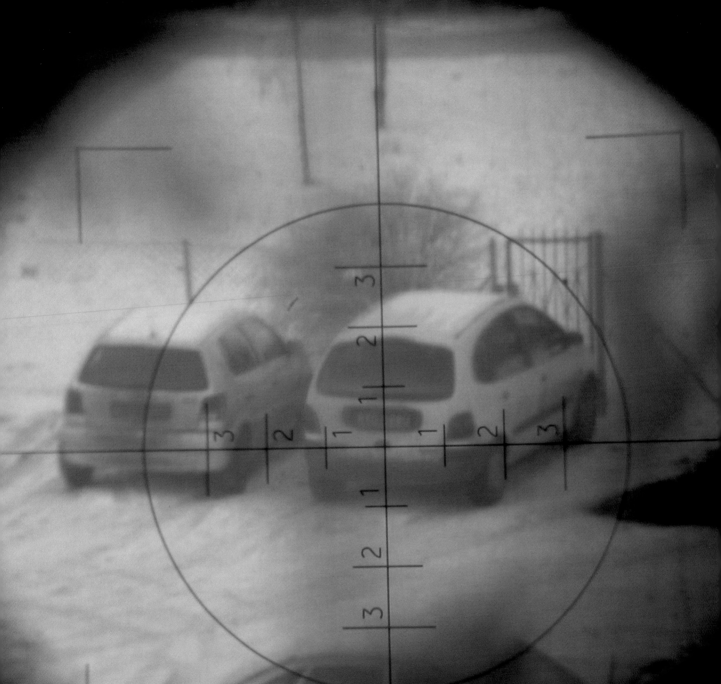

The United Nations works to make the world secure from the violence of terrorism.

Chapter

6

International Law and Terrorism

Terrorism is nothing new. In fact, it has been around for hundreds of years. The word "terrorist" was first used during the French Revolution in the 1790s to describe those carrying out mass executions of the aristocracy. Modern terrorism, with surprise attacks against civilians, became more common during the nineteenth century, as Irish **nationalists** fought for an Ireland independent of Great Britain.

Artist Francisco de Goya portrayed the horrors of terrorism during the French invasion of Spain in the early nineteenth century.

Defining Terrorism

The simple definition of terrorism is the act of causing fear, through violence or the threat of violence, to create political pressure on a group or government. For political reasons, however, member countries of the United Nations have found it difficult to agree on a single definition of terrorism. For example, if the definition states that terrorist acts are carried out against civilians, this would exclude any attacks against military personnel or targets, even if those attacks were not carried out during wartime.

In 1937, the League of Nations began trying to put together an acceptable definition of terrorism. Its definition stated that terrorism was, "all criminal acts directed against a State and intended or calculated to create a state of terror in the minds of particular persons or a group of persons or the general public." With the beginning of World War II in 1939, though, and the eventual breakup of the League of Nations, this definition was never formally adopted.

In 1994, the Declaration on Measures to Eliminate International Terrorism stated that crimes of terrorism are:

From Resolution 1373

Acting under Chapter VII of the Charter of the United Nations,

1. *Decides* that all States shall:

(a) Prevent and suppress the financing of terrorist acts. . . .

2. *Decides* also that all States shall:

(a) Refrain from providing any form of support, active or passive, to entities or persons involved in terrorist acts, including by suppressing recruitment of members of terrorist groups and eliminating the supply of weapons to terrorists;

(b) Take the necessary steps to prevent the commission of terrorist acts, including by provision of early warning to other States by exchange of information;

(c) Deny safe haven to those who finance, plan, support, or commit terrorist acts, or provide safe havens. . . .

(g) Prevent the movement of terrorists or terrorist groups by effective border controls and controls on issuance of identity papers and travel documents, and through measures for preventing counterfeiting, forgery or fraudulent use of identity papers and travel documents. . . .

Criminal acts intended or calculated to provoke a state of terror in the general public, a group of persons or particular persons for political purposes are in any circumstance unjustifiable, whatever the considerations of a political, philosophical, ***ideological***, racial, ethnic, religious or any other nature that may be invoked to justify them.

While definitions similar to this have been used in a number of UN resolutions and declarations against terrorism, still no single definition of terrorism has been agreed upon.

Some leaders have proposed that the United Nations issue a comprehensive Convention against Terrorism, tying together the issues addressed in the other existing treaties, but this would require international agreement on a definition of terrorism. One terrorism expert has proposed defining an act of terrorism simply as the "peacetime equivalent of a war crime," but this has yet to be adopted.

The Terrorism Prevention Branch

Terrorism has been a concern of the United Nations for nearly as long as the organization has existed. During the twentieth century, the United Nations and other groups drafted international treaties to address terrorist activities as incidents occurred. By the 1990s, terrorist attacks had become a common way for small ***radical*** groups to try and force governments to give in to their demands. In response, the United Nations formed the Terrorism Prevention Branch, a group serving under the authority of the UNODC.

The purpose of the Terrorism Prevention Branch is to assist nations in reaching agreements on measures to be taken against terrorist activities. The group keeps a ***database*** of all terrorist incidents and works to calculate the threats of further attacks. Their goals include helping countries prevent terrorist attacks, control attacks as they happen, and recover after attacks. The Terrorism Prevention Branch works closely with the Centre for International Crime Prevention in all these tasks.

The Counter-Terrorism Committee

Late in September of 2001, in response to the September 11 terrorist attacks against the World Trade Center in New York City and the Pentagon in Washington, D.C., the United Nations issued Resolution 1373, a Mandatory Action to Fight Terrorism. This resolution expanded on Resolution 1368, issued the day after the attacks, that specifically addressed the September 11 attacks and

Terrorism Conventions

United Nations Conventions

- Convention on the Prevention and Punishment of Crimes against Internationally Protected Persons, including Diplomatic Agents: 1973
- International Convention against the Taking of Hostages: 1979
- International Convention for the Suppression of Terrorist Bombings: 1997
- International Convention for the Suppression of the Financing of Terrorism: 1999
- International Convention for the Suppression of Acts of Nuclear Terrorism: 2005

Other International Organizations Conventions

- Convention on Offences and Certain Other Acts Committed on Board Aircraft: 1963 (International Civil Aviation Organization)
- Convention for the Suppression of Unlawful Seizure of Aircraft: 1970 (Governments of the Russian Federation, the United Kingdom and the United States of America)
- Convention for the Suppression of Unlawful Acts against the Safety of Civil Aviation: 1971 (Governments of the Russian Federation, the United Kingdom and the United States of America)
- Convention on the Physical Protection of Nuclear Material: 1980 (International Atomic Energy Agency)
- Protocol on the Suppression of Unlawful Acts of Violence at Airports Serving International Civil Aviation, supplementary to the Convention for the Suppression of Unlawful Acts against the Safety of Civil Aviation: 1988 (Governments of the Russian Federation, the United Kingdom and the United States of America and the International Civil Aviation Organization)
- Convention for the Suppression of Unlawful Acts against the Safety of Maritime Navigation: 1988 (International Maritime Organization)
- Protocol for the Suppression of Unlawful Acts against the Safety of Fixed Platforms Located on the Continental Shelf: 1988 (International Maritime Organization)
- Convention on the Marking of Plastic Explosives for the Purpose of Detection: 1991 (International Civil Aviation Organization)

Regional Conventions

- OAS Convention to Prevent and Punish Acts of Terrorism Taking the Form of Crimes against Persons and Related Extortion that are of International

Significance: 1971 (Organization of American States)
- SAARC Regional Convention on Suppression of Terrorism: 1987 (South Asian Association for Regional Cooperation)
- European Convention on the Suppression of Terrorism: 1997 (Council of Europe)
- Arab Convention on the Suppression of Terrorism: 1998 (League of Arab States)
- Convention of the Organization of the Islamic Conference on Combating International Terrorism: 1999 (Organization of the Islamic Conference)
- OAU Convention on the Prevention and Combating of Terrorism: 1999 (the Organization of African Unity)
- Treaty on Cooperation among States Members of the Commonwealth of Independent States in Combating Terrorism: 1999 (Commonwealth of Independent States)

called on member nations "to work together urgently to bring to justice the perpetrators, organizers and sponsors of these terrorist attacks."

Resolution 1373, while condemning terrorism in general and appealing to UN member countries to crack down on terrorist activities, also established the Counter-Terrorism Committee (CTC). The purpose of the CTC is not to track terrorist activities—the job of the Terrorism Prevention Branch—but to make sure the member nations follow the decisions laid out in Resolution 1373. These decisions include freezing the funds of known terrorist groups and refusing to shelter wanted terrorists. In 2004, the UN Security Council agreed to renew the mission of the CTC and added the Counter-Terrorism Committee Executive Directorate (CTED), a group of experts working with and assisting the CTC.

Conventions on Terrorism

Since its creation, the United Nations has either created, or supported the creation of, a number of international treaties on various aspects of terrorism. In 1963, the International Civil Aviation Organization (ICAO) drafted the Convention on Offences and Certain Other Acts Committed On Board Aircraft. The first terrorism-related convention drafted by the United Nations was the Convention on the Prevention and Punishment of Crimes against Internationally Protected

In the twenty-first century, the United Nations is directing more attention and effort to curbing terrorists than ever before.

Pioneering International Law: Conventions, Treaties, and Standards

Persons, including diplomatic agents, adopted in 1973. Since then, the United Nations has adopted four more international treaties related to terrorism, and many countries have ratified fourteen other terrorism-related conventions drafted by international or regional organizations.

Since there are so many different conventions associated with antiterrorism, some political experts have suggested they be replaced with a single international treaty. This would take a great deal of work and cooperation on the part of the signing countries; many have signed certain conventions but not others. To adopt a single convention on terrorism, the majority of UN member countries would need to agree on all the points, including a comprehensive definition of terrorism.

The American War on Terrorism

On September 11, 2001, the terrorist group al-Qaeda hijacked four American airplanes. The hijackers flew two of the planes into the World Trade Center in New York City. One flew into the Pentagon outside of Washington, D.C., and the fourth crashed into a field in Pennsylvania. Shortly

On September 11, 2001, the United States suffered an attack from the terrorist group al Qaeda.

after the attacks, U.S. president George W. Bush declared a "war on terror" against the group that had carried out the attack, all other terrorist groups, and the countries that harbored these groups. The UN Security Council, in a resolution issued on September 12, stated that the Security Council "expresses its readiness to take all necessary steps to respond to the terrorist attacks of 11 September 2001, and to combat all forms of terrorism, in accordance with its responsibilities under the Charter of the United Nations."

Since the leader of al-Qaeda, Osama bin Laden, was known to live in Afghanistan, both the United Nations and the United States issued demands for the Taliban—the government leading the country—to turn over bin Laden for prosecution. When the Taliban refused, an American-led coalition of forces launched attacks on Afghanistan, with approximately twenty countries contributing assistance. By the next year, the Taliban had been thrown out of power (although bin Laden was not found).

The United Nations began a political mission to Afghanistan in March of 2002, called the UN Assistance Mission in Afghanistan (UNAMA). The purpose of the mission is to help the country rebuild from war and from years under the restrictive policies of the Taliban government.

In March of 2003, the United States began an invasion of Iraq. The U.S. government believed the Iraqi government, under the leadership of Saddam Hussein, was hiding weapons of mass destruction, such as chemical or biological weapons. The United Nations did not give its consent to the invasion of Iraq and considered it illegal. The United States contended that Proposition 1441, passed in November 2002, provided firm legal basis for the war, although the United States never officially declared it a war. The proposition listed a number of actions that Iraq had to perform or else "face serious consequences as a result of its continued violations of its obligations." The capital city of Baghdad fell in April of 2003, and the next month, President Bush stated that major combat missions in Iraq were over. However, American occupation continued. No weapons of mass destruction were ever found. This, and the fact that the United Nations condemned the invasion, has led some to call for an investigation of America's actions by the International Criminal Court.

The United Nations has always denounced terrorism. Terrorist acts directly defy the principles of the United Nations, which call for international peace and security, as well as "better standards of life." To this end, the United Nations has worked to establish international treaties and conventions that would unite the world in the fight against terrorism.

Many conventions drafted by the United Nations have become international law, ratified by numerous countries. While the United Nations has an enormous influence with the creation of international law, the effectiveness of these laws depends on the cooperation of the signing nations. As long as countries are willing to follow the treaties established by the United Nations, the system of international law works well.

Time Line

1864	First Geneva Convention is held.
1899	First Hague Convention is held.
1899	Permanent Court of Arbitration is established.
1925	The Geneva Protocol bans chemical and biological weapons.
1945	The United Nations is founded.
1945	Creation of the International Court of Justice.
1947	UN International Law Commission is founded.
1948	First UN peacekeeping mission.
1948	Centre for International Crime Prevention is founded.
1955	First UN Crime Congress is held.
1956	United Nations Emergency Force becomes first modern peacekeeping mission.
1992	Commission on Crime Prevention and Criminal Justice is created.
1994	United Nations Convention on the Law of the Sea goes into effect.
1994	International Seabed Authority is established.
1994	International Tribunal for the Law of the Sea is established.
1997	UN Office on Drugs and Crime is founded.
2001	Counter-Terrorism Committee is established.

2002	United Nations World Summit on Sustainable Development stresses need for protection of oceans and marine life.
June 25, 2005	International Day against Drug Abuse and Illicit Trafficking.
December 9, 2005	International Anti-Corruption Day.
2006	The United Nations continues to fight international crime.

Glossary

amelioration: The act of improving something.

appeal: A formal request to a higher authority requesting a change of a decision.

arbitral tribunals: Legal groups appointed to make judgments in arbitration cases (see below).

arbitration: The process of resolving disputes between people or groups by referring them to a third party either agreed on by them or provided by law.

breaches: Failures to obey.

codification: The act of arranging laws, rules, or codes of behavior into organized systems.

conciliation: Action taken to reach agreement or to restore trust.

continental shelf: A submerged border of a continent that slopes gradually to a steeper slope to the ocean bottom.

database: A systematically arranged collection of computer data, structured so that it can be automatically retrieved or manipulated.

diplomatic: Having to do with international negotiations without resort to violence.

extradition: The handing over by a government of someone accused of a crime in a different country for trial or punishment where the crime was committed.

flag of parley: A white flag waved to indicate the desire to negotiate.

ideological: Based on a closely organized system of beliefs, values, and ideas forming the basis of a social, economic, or political philosophy.

money laundering: The practice of engaging in financial transactions in order to conceal the identity, source, and/or destination of money.

nationalists: Those with an extreme sense of loyalty to their country.

nautical miles: Iinternational units of measurement of distance at sea, equal to approximately 6,076 feet (1.852 kilometers).

polymetallic nodules: Porous objects of various sizes and shapes, found in thin shallow layers on the floor of the ocean.

preventive: Used to stop something from happening.

radical: Extreme in behavior or beliefs.

ratify: Formally approve.

sanctions: Punishments imposed as a result of breaking a rule or law.

stereotypes: Generalizations based on incomplete and often inaccurate information.

summit: A meeting between heads of government or other high-ranking officials to discuss something of great importance.

veto: The power of one country or branch of government to reject the legislation of another.

Further Reading

Balkin, Karen. *The War on Terrorism.* San Diego, Calif.: Greenhaven Press, 2004.

Driscoll, William, Joseph Zompetti, and Suzette W. Zompetti, eds. *The International Criminal Court: Global Politics and the Quest for Justice.* New York: International Debate Education Association, 2004.

Katz, Samuel M. *Global Counterstrike: International Counterterrorism.* Minneapolis, Minn.: Lerner Publishing Group, 2004.

Kolba, Boris. *International Courts.* Milwaukee, Wis.: World Almanac Library, 2003.

Townsend, John. *Organized Crime.* Oxford, United Kingdom: Raintree, 2005.

For More Information

International Court of Justice
www.icj-cij.org/icjwww/icj002.htm

International Law Commission
www.un.org/law/ilc/introfra.htm

Maritime Law History
www.historyoflaw.info/maritime-law-history.html

Oceans and the Law of the Sea
www.un.org/Depts/los/index.htm

Preventative Diplomacy
www.un.org/Depts/dpa/prev_dip/fst_prev_dip.htm

Terrorism Prevention Branch
www.uncjin.org/CICP/terror

United Nations Action against Terrorism
www.un.org/terrorism

United Nations and International Law
www.un.org/law

United Nations Office on Drugs and Crime
www.unodc.org/unodc/index.html

United Nations Peacekeeping
www.un.org/Depts/dpko/dpko/index.asp

Reports and Projects

Research and write a report about one of the cases currently being considered by the International Court of Justice. What are the views of those on each side? What do you think the court should decide?

How have international laws made a difference in the world? Write about a situation that has improved because of an international law treaty.

Imagine you are a UN peacekeeper. Research a current UN peacekeeping mission and write a journal entry describing some of the experiences you might have.

Do a class presentation on the differences between ancient and modern pirates.

With a group, study one aspect of international crime facing the world today. Tell the class about what you have discovered.

Bibliography

Bolton, Sally. "Peacekeeping and Conflict Resolution: Then and Now." *UN Chronicle Online Edition.* 2005. http://www.un.org/Pubs/chronicle/2005/webArticles/101705_peacekeeping.html.

Carnegie Foundation. *The Peace Palace.* 2003. http://www.vredespaleis.nl/showpage.asp?pag_id=1.

Centre for International Crime Prevention. "Global Programmes." http://www.uncjin.org/CICP/Folder/front.htm.

Centre for International Crime Prevention. http://www.uncjin.org/CICP/cicp.html.

"China Adopts UN Convention Against Corruption." *News from Russia.* November 10, 2005. http://newsfromrussia.com/world/2005/11/10/67375.html.

Codification Division, Office of Legal Affairs, United Nations. *International Law Commission.* 1998. http://www.un.org/law/ilc/introfra.htm.

Conflict Research Consortium. "Peacebuilding—Official Efforts of UN and Regional Organizations." *International Online Training Program on Intractable Conflict.* http://www.colorado.edu/conflict/peace/treatment/peacebld.htm.

"Convention for the Amelioration of the Condition of the Wounded in Armies in the Field, Geneva, 22 August 1864." *International Humanitarian Law-Treaties and Documents.* 2005. http://www.icrc.org/ihl.nsf/385ec082b509e76c41256739003e636d/87a3bb58c1c44f0dc125641a005a06e0?OpenDocument.

Council on Environmental Quality. "Vice President Al Gore Announces New Action to Help Protect and Preserve U.S. Shores and Oceans." 1999. http://clinton4.nara.gov/CEQ/990902a.html.

Counter Terrorism Committee, UN Action Against Terrorism. 2003. http://www.un.org/Docs/sc/committees/1373.

Crime.org. http://www.crime.org/links.html.

Division of Ocean Affairs and the Law of the Sea, Office of Legal Affairs, United Nations. *Oceans and Law of the Sea.* 2005. http://www.un.org/Depts/los/index.htm.

Division of Ocean Affairs and the Law of the Sea, Office of Legal Affairs, United Nations. *Settlement of Disputes Mechanism.* 2005. http://www.un.org/Depts/los/settlement_of_disputes/choice_procedure.htm.

Division of Ocean Affairs and the Law of the Sea, Office of Legal Affairs, United Nations. *The United Nations Convention on the Law of the Sea—A Historical Perspective.* 1998. http://www.un.org/Depts/los/convention_agreements/convention_historical_perspective.htm#Historical%20Perspective.

Geanakoplos, Deno. "Prologue: The Two Worlds of Christendom-Administration, Political Theory, Law and Diplomacy." *Myriobiblos Library.* http://www.myriobiblos.gr/texts/english/geanakoplos_twoworlds_7.html.

Hacken, Richard, and Jane Plotke. "Hague Convention." *World War I Document Archive.* 2005. http://www.lib.byu.edu/~rdh/wwi/hague.html.

"History of Admiralty Law." *Maritime Legal Resources.* http://www.marlegal.com/mlhist.html.

IIMCR: The Institute for International Mediation and Conflict Resolution. 2005. http://www.iimcr.org.

INCORE: International Conflict Research. 2004. http://www.incore.ulst.ac.uk.

International Civil Aviation Organization. http://www.icao.int.

International Seabed Authority. *Structure and Functioning.* http://www.isa.org.jm/en/seabedarea/TechBrochures/ENG2.pdf.

"Maritime Law." Brent Adams and Associates, Personal Injury Lawyers. http://www.ncpersonalinjurylaw.com/maritime-attorneys-north-carolina.php.

"Maritime Law History." *History of Law.* http://www.historyoflaw.info/maritime-law-history.html.

Nonviolent Peaceforce. 2005. http://nvpf.org/np/english/welcome.asp.html.

Permanent Court of Arbitration. 2005. http://pca-cpa.org/ENGLISH/GI/.

"Preventative Diplomacy." United Nations Department of Political Affairs. http://www.un.org/Depts/dpa/prev_dip/fst_prev_dip.htm.

"Security Council Restructures Counter-Terrorism Committee, to Strengthen Implementation of 2001 Anti-Terrorism Resolution." March 26, 2004. http://www.un.org/News/Press/docs/2004/sc8041.doc.htm.

Society of Professional Journalists. *Reference Guide to the Geneva Conventions.* 2002. http://www.genevaconventions.org.

Terrorism Prevention Branch, United Nations Office for Drug Control and Crime Prevention. http://www.uncjin.org/CICP/terror.

"Text of the Biological and Toxin Weapons Convention." Biological and Toxin Weapons Convention Database. http://www.brad.ac.uk/acad/sbtwc/keytext/genprot.htm.

United Nations Action Against Terrorism. http://www.un.org/terrorism.

United Nations Crime and Justice Information Network. http://www.uncjin.org.

United Nations Department of Peacekeeping Operations. "Mission Statement." 2005. http://www.un.org/Depts/dpko/dpko/info/page3.htm.

United Nations Department of Public Information. United Nations Crime Congresses. 1995. http://www.un.org/ecosocdev/geninfo/crime/dpi1643e.htm.

United Nations Information Service. "Country Visits Signal New Phase of Work for United Nations Counter-Terrorism Body." March 15, 2005. http://www.unis.unvienna.org/unis/pressrels/2005/sc8333.html.

United Nations International Law. http://www.un.org/law.

United Nations Office for Drug Control and Crime Prevention. "The Terrorism Prevention Branch." http://www.uncjin.org/Special/PM991216/Netscape/WebTPB.htm.

United Nations Office on Drugs and Crime. "Commission on Crime Prevention and Criminal Justice." http://www.unodc.org/unodc/en/crime_cicp_commission.html.

United Nations Office on Drugs and Crime. http://www.unodc.org/unodc/index.html.

United Nations Peace and Security. http://www.un.org/peace.

United Nations Peacekeeping. http://www.un.org/Depts/dpko/dpko/index.asp.

UN General Assembly "Measures to Eliminate International Terrorism." December 9, 1994. http://www.un.org/documents/ga/res/49/a49r060.htm.

"UN Security Council Mandatory Action to Fight Terrorism." September 28, 2001. http://www.staff.city.ac.uk/p.willetts/TERROR/SC-1373.HTM.

"UN Security Council Resolution 1269 on Terrorism." October 19, 1999. http://www.un.int/usa/sres1269.htm.

"UN Security Council Resolution 1368." September 12, 2001. http://www.state.gov/p/io/rls/othr/2001/4899.htm.

"US Says Iraq Invasion was Legal." BBC News. September 16, 2004. http://news.bbc.co.uk/2/hi/middle_east/3664234.stm.

Index

Picture Credits

Corel (United Nations): pp. 9, 11, 13, 14, 15, 25, 28, 30, 32, 33, 34
iStock:
    Dan Schmidt: p. 49
    Lauren Rinder: p. 57
    Lisa Kyle Young: p. 12
    Maciej Sekowski: p. 64
    Michael Osterrieder: p. 44
    Oleksandr Gumerov: p. 71
    Roel Hoyer: p. 16
    Shayna Marchese: p. 4
Jupiter Images: pp. 38, 43, 47, 50, 52, 56, 58, 60, 61, 62
Permanent Court of Arbitration: p. 24
Relief Web: p. 36
UNICEF: p. 35

To the best knowledge of the publisher, all other images are in the public domain. If any image has been inadvertently uncredited, please notify Harding House Publishing Service, Vestal, New York 13850, so that rectification can be made for future printings.

Biographies

Author

Sheila Nelson has written a number of educational books for young people. She lives in Rochester, New York, with her husband and children.

Series Consultant

Bruce Russett is Dean Acheson Professor of Political Science at Yale University and editor of the *Journal of Conflict Resolution*. He has taught or researched at Columbia, Harvard, M.I.T., Michigan, and North Carolina in the United States, and educational institutions in Belgium, Britain, Israel, Japan, and the Netherlands. He has been president of the International Studies Association and the Peace Science Society, holds an honorary doctorate from Uppsala University in Sweden. He was principal adviser to the U.S. Catholic Bishops for their pastoral letter on nuclear deterrence in 1985, and co-directed the staff for the 1995 Ford Foundation Report, *The United Nations in Its Second Half Century.* He has served as editor of the *Journal of Conflict Resolution* since 1973. The twenty-five books he has published include *The Once and Future Security Council* (1997), *Triangulating Peace: Democracy, Interdependence, and International Organizations* (2001), *World Politics: The Menu for Choice* (8th edition 2006), and *Purpose and Policy in the Global Community* (2006).